W9-AVT-058

3 3090 00584 1848

Should Girls PLAY SPORTS with Boys?

By Amy B. Rogers

FREMONT PUBLIC LIBRARY DISTRICT WITHDRAWN
1170 N. Midlothian Road
Mundelein, IL 60060

KidHaven
PUBLISHING

Published in 2018 by
KidHaven Publishing, an Imprint of Greenhaven Publishing, LLC
353 3rd Avenue
Suite 255
New York, NY 10010

Copyright © 2018 KidHaven Publishing, an Imprint of Greenhaven Publishing, LLC.

All rights reserved. No part of this book may be reproduced in any form without permission in writing from the publisher, except by a reviewer.

Designer: Seth Hughes
Editor: Katie Kawa

Photo credits: Cover © iStockphoto.com/FatCamera; p. 5 (top) © iStockphoto.com/monkeybusinessimages; p. 5 (bottom) Purestock/Thinkstock; p. 7 AP Photo/Jeff Chiu; pp. 9 (left), 21 (notepad) ESB Professional/Shutterstock.com; p. 9 (right) filipefrazao/iStock/Thinkstock; p. 11 wavebreakmedia/Shutterstock.com; p. 13 KidStock/Blend Images/Getty Images; p. 15 Jared Wickerham/Getty Images; p. 17 (top) Creatas Images/Creatas/Thinkstock; pp. 17 (bottom), 21 (inset, middle-right) Jupiterimages/Stockbyte/Thinkstock; p. 19 Jupiterimages/Goodshoot/Thinkstock; p. 20 Action Sports Photography/Shutterstock.com; p. 21 (markers) Kucher Serhii/Shutterstock.com; p. 21 (photo frame) FARBAI/iStock/Thinkstock; p. 21 (inset, left) Valueline/Thinkstock; p. 21 (inset, middle-left) Ryan McVay/Photodisc/Thinkstock; p. 21 (inset, right) moodboard/Thinkstock.

Cataloging-in-Publication Data

Names: Rogers, Amy B.
Title: Should girls play sports with boys? / Amy B. Rogers.
Description: New York : KidHaven Publishing, 2018. | Series: Points of view | Includes glossary and index.
Identifiers: ISBN 9781534524835 (pbk.) | 9781534524217 (library bound) | ISBN 9781534524842 (6 pack) | ISBN 9781534524224 (ebook)
Subjects: LCSH: United States. Education Amendments of 1972. Title IX–Juvenile literature. | Sex discrimination in sports–United States–Juvenile literature. | Women athletes–Legal status, laws, etc.–United States–Juvenile literature.
Classification: LCC KF4166.R64 2018 | DDC 344.73'099–dc23

Printed in the United States of America

CPSIA compliance information: Batch #CW18KL: For further information contact Greenhaven Publishing LLC, New York, New York at 1-844-317-7404.

Please visit our website, www.greenhavenpublishing.com. For a free color catalog of all our high-quality books, call toll free 1-844-317-7404 or fax 1-844-317-7405.

CONTENTS

Better
TOGETHER?

Girls and boys like to play sports with their friends. They play on teams for their town or their school. Sometimes, these teams are made up of all boys or all girls. Other times, these teams let boys and girls play together.

Some people don't think girls and boys should play sports together. They worry girls might get hurt. Other people think it's good to let girls and boys see that they're equals on the same team. These groups have different points of view. It's good to understand different points of view before deciding how you feel about an issue.

Know the Facts!

Girls have been allowed to play Little League Baseball with boys since 1974.

Do you think girls and boys should play sports together or on separate teams? Knowing all the facts on both sides of a **debate** helps you have an informed, or educated, opinion.

A Game-Changing
LAW

For many years, girls who wanted to play sports weren't treated the same as boys. Then, a law was passed in 1972 called Title IX, or Title Nine. This law states schools that get money from the **federal** government have to give girls and women the same opportunities to play sports that they give boys and men.

This law led to an increase in girls and women playing sports. Young girls began to see more women playing sports in college and **professionally**. This made them want to start playing sports, too—both on all-girls teams and on teams with boys.

Know the Facts!

Title IX helped women's sports grow like never before. Before Title IX was passed, around 1 out of every 27 girls played sports in high school. Today, that number is around two out of every five girls.

In 2016, the Sonoma Stompers signed three female baseball players to their **roster**. Kelsie Whitmore (right), Stacy Piagno (left), and Anna Kimbrell became the first female teammates on a professional baseball team in more than 50 years.

UNSAFE

One of the biggest worries people have about girls playing sports with boys is that girls could get hurt. When boys and girls are young, their bodies aren't very different. However, as they grow up, their bodies change.

Men generally grow to be taller and heavier than women. Their bodies can support more muscle. People worry that it wouldn't just be unfair to ask women to **compete** against taller, stronger men—it would be unsafe. Separating male and female athletes from a young age means this never becomes a problem.

Know the Facts!

Men's red blood cells have more hemoglobin, which carries oxygen through the body, than women's red blood cells. Scientists think having more hemoglobin can help men run faster.

Because male athletes are generally taller and heavier than female athletes, they are often stronger. This has caused some people to worry that female athletes could get hurt playing against male athletes in sports such as football, hockey, or soccer.

Not So
DIFFERENT

There are important differences between male and female athletes. However, those differences don't generally exist between young boys and girls. Scientists have stated that there's no reason to believe young girls are **physically** weaker than boys of the same age or that their bones can break more easily.

Because of this, many people argue that there's no scientific reason why young boys and girls need to play on different sports teams. They can be separated when they get older if the differences between their bodies begin to cause problems.

Know the Facts!

One study of young swimmers found there was no difference between girls and boys under 8 years old in terms of how fast they swam.

Girls are often as tall and strong as boys when they're younger. In some cases, girls are actually taller and stronger than the boys on their team!

BULLIES

Some people worry about more than girls' bodies getting hurt if they play with boys. They think it could be harmful for them in other ways, too. Girls might be bullied by kids who think they don't belong on the same team as boys. This often happens when they face another team made up of only boys.

Parents can be bullies, too. They might say mean things about a girl they don't want playing with their sons. They might even try to keep a girl from joining a team.

Know the Facts!

More than 25,000 girls play youth football, according to USA Football.

Schools sometimes try to keep girls from joining boys' teams, such as football teams. Parents have gone to court to fight for their daughters' rights to play football with boys.

EQUAL

Although bullying is an important concern, many people argue that girls shouldn't be kept from playing sports with boys out of fear. In fact, girls who play on boys' sports teams often say they're treated well by their teammates.

Allowing girls and boys to play on the same team teaches young people to respect each other. They learn that what should matter is a person's skills and not whether they're a boy or girl. This helps boys and girls to see each other as equals, which is a good lesson to learn at a young age.

Know the Facts!

Around 100,000 girls play youth baseball, but that number drops to around 1,200 once they reach high school.

Mo'ne Davis became famous in 2014 as the first girl to pitch a winning game in the Little League World Series. She helped more people see that girls could have fun and be very successful playing sports with boys.

LONELY

Letting girls and boys play on the same sports teams can help kids learn to work together. However, even if the teammates all get along, there will always be some kind of separation between boys and girls.

Boys and girls have separate locker rooms and other places to change. This makes it hard for them to all feel as if they're part of the same team all the time. If there's only one girl on a team, she might feel lonely. She has to get ready for a game and spend time after a game by herself.

Know the Facts!

In 1978, a female sports reporter named Melissa Ludtke went to court to fight for her right to **interview** male players in their locker room, and she won.

Being the only girl on a team can be hard. Some athletes would rather play on an all-girls team so they can be around other girls.

CONFIDENCE

If a girl wants to play a sport on an all-boys team, many people believe she should be **encouraged**. Telling an athlete she can't play on a team because she's a girl teaches her to limit herself.

It's important for girls to grow up believing in themselves. This is called having confidence. Playing sports can help build confidence. Studies have shown that being on a team with boys helps girls grow up to be tough and strong. It can also help girls work even harder to get better at their sport.

Know the Facts!

Playing sports helps both boys and girls stay healthy and do well in school. Studies have also shown that young athletes are less likely to use drugs than kids who don't play sports.

Many times, girls say the fight to be able to play sports with boys and be respected for their skills has made them more confident. This is important because many girls struggle with confidence as they get older.

POINT OF VIEW

Have you played on a sports team with both boys and girls? If you have, then your personal **experiences** can help you form your point of view about boys and girls playing sports together.

Personal experiences help shape our point of view, and so does learning about other opinions and new facts. After learning why people feel the way they do about girls and boys playing sports together, what do you think? Should girls play sports with boys, should they always be separated, or should it depend on the girls, the boys, and the team?

Know the Facts!

Auto racing is one sport in which women compete against men professionally. Danica Patrick is one famous female driver.

Should girls play sports with boys?

YES

- The bodies of boys and girls aren't different when they're kids, which means it's safe and fair for them to play together.

- Girls and boys playing sports together teaches lessons about equality and respect.

- Playing sports with boys gives girls confidence.

NO

- The differences between men's and women's bodies will make playing some sports together unsafe and unfair when they grow up, and separation keeps it from becoming an issue.

- Girls can be bullied by kids and parents for playing on boys' teams.

- Playing sports with boys can be lonely for girls.

This chart can help you remember the different arguments for and against girls playing sports with boys as you form your own opinion.

GLOSSARY

compete: To try to win something that someone else is also trying to win.

debate: An argument or discussion about an issue, generally between two sides.

encourage: To make someone more likely to do something.

experience: Skill or knowledge someone gets by doing something.

federal: Relating to the central government of the United States.

interview: A meeting at which someone gets information from a person.

physical: Relating to the body.

professional: Having to do with a job someone does for a living.

roster: A list of people who belong to a team.

For More
INFORMATION

WEBSITES

"5 Reasons Girls Should Play Sports"

kidshealth.org/en/kids/5-sports.html#catdieting
This KidsHealth article gives girls information on the ways playing sports—with or without boys—can be good for them.

Little League

www.littleleague.org/Little_League_Online.htm
The official Little League website features information for boys and girls who want to play baseball for this organization.

BOOKS

Colich, Abby. *Danica Patrick*. North Mankato, MN: Pebble Plus, 2016.

Davis, Mo'Ne, and Hilary Beard. *Remember My Name: My Story from First Pitch to Game Changer*. New York, NY: HarperCollins, 2015.

Stabler, David, and Doogie Horner. *Kid Athletes: True Tales of Childhood from Sports Legends*. Philadelphia, PA: Quirk Books, 2015.

Publisher's note to educators and parents: Our editors have carefully reviewed these websites to ensure that they are suitable for students. Many websites change frequently, however, and we cannot guarantee that a site's future contents will continue to meet our high standards of quality and educational value. Be advised that students should be closely supervised whenever they access the Internet.

INDEX